W9-BSF-398

WEATHER
FORECASTING

By Marcie Aboff

CELEBRATION PRESS
Pearson Learning Group

Contents

All Kinds of Weather

How do you know if you should wear a jacket to school? How do you know if it might snow? You check the weather **forecast**! A forecast tells what the weather will be like.

Weather is the condition of the air in a certain place. Air temperature, **humidity**, rain, snow, and wind are all part of the weather. Weather changes because the condition of the air changes. In this book, you will learn about some ways in which information about the weather is collected and studied. The information is used to make weather forecasts.

Did you ever have a snow day? People use weather forecasts to decide whether or not to close schools.

Forecasting the Weather

Who says what the weather will be like tomorrow? That is the job of meteorologists. Meteorologists are weather watchers. They study and predict the weather. They use many tools to make weather forecasts.

Weather **conditions** are measured all around the world every day. Weather information is usually collected a few times a day. The **data** comes from tools in space, in the air, and on the ground. Meteorologists use computers to study the data.

a meteorologist studying weather data

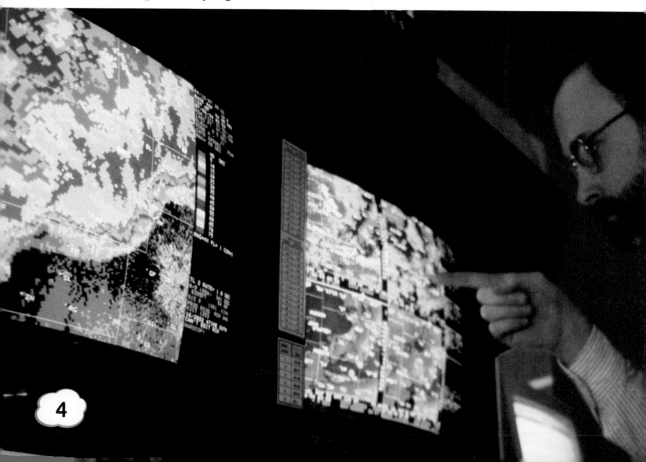

FRI	48	☁☀	63
SAT	46	☀☁	65
SUN	48	☀☁ North	64
MON	46	☀	65
TUE	47	☀	66

A meteorologist can predict the weather for several days.

The next step is to make a prediction. Meteorologists look at the information they have gathered. They **compare** it to past weather patterns. They think about what kind of weather the air conditions have caused in the past.

This information is used to predict what the weather will be like. Weather can usually be predicted for up to five days at a time. The chances are greater for a change in weather when predictions are made more than 3 days in advance.

Measuring Weather High in the Sky

What kinds of instruments **record** weather data? Some of the instruments are **satellites** that **orbit** Earth. They record information about cloud cover, storms, and other weather conditions. The information is sent to meteorologists to be studied.

Weather satellites take pictures of clouds and show where storms are forming.

satellite image showing a strong hurricane heading toward the coast

Radar

Radar is an important weather tool. Radar works by sending out bursts of radio waves from an antenna. The waves bounce off raindrops, snowflakes, and other objects. Computers review the waves that bounce back. How strong are the waves? How long did they take to travel? Computers use this information to tell where rain and snow are falling. Radar can also be used to find out the speed of wind.

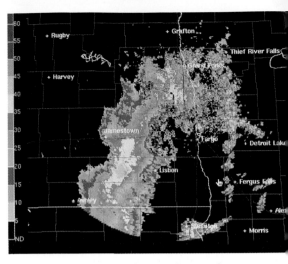

The colored dots from the radar show where the rain is.

Weather Balloons

Weather balloons carry instruments high in the air. The instruments measure temperature, **air pressure**, and humidity. The balloons will burst when they reach 90,000 feet. A parachute floats the instruments to the ground.

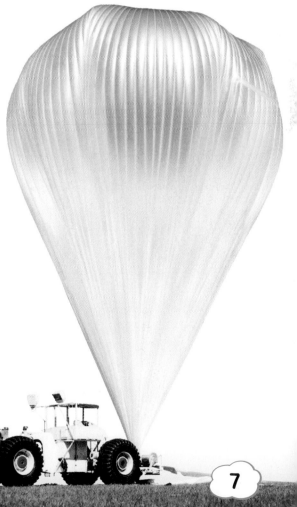

A weather balloon flies for about two hours.

Measuring Weather on the Ground

Temperature, wind speed, air pressure, and humidity are measured daily from the ground. Who takes these measurements? Weather watchers at the National Weather Service (NWS) do. The NWS has weather stations all around the country. Any rain or snow that falls is also measured.

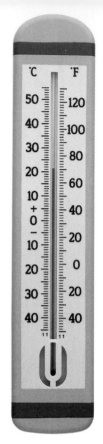

This thermometer measures degrees Fahrenheit and Celsius. Water freezes at 32 degrees Fahrenheit and at 0 degrees Celsius.

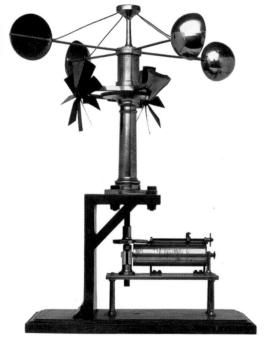

an anemometer, used to measure wind speeds

Weather Instruments

Temperature is measured in degrees. Wind speed is measured in miles per hour. Air pressure is measured in inches! That's because instruments that measure air pressure hold liquid. The liquid rises or falls as air presses on it. High pressure usually means a clear day. Pressure that is low or falling may mean wet weather is on the way.

Snow Stick

Meteorologists have a simple way to measure snow. They place a measuring stick into the snow! Sometimes the wind blows the snow into drifts. So, the snow is measured in more than one place. Then, the measurements are averaged.

You can measure the depth of snow with a ruler.

a barometer, used to measure air pressure

Weather Averages

Snow is measured in three different places. The meteorologist may measure 6, 4, and 5 inches. The numbers are added to get 15 inches. This total number is divided by the number of measurements taken: $15 \div 3 = 5$. So, 5 inches is the average snowfall.

Meteorologists also average rainfall and temperatures. These averages are recorded over the years. They help forecasters know what the weather should be like at different times of the year.

Stratus clouds are low, gray clouds. They form about 5,000 feet above the ground.

Cumulus clouds are white and puffy. They form 5,000 to 20,000 feet above the ground.

Cirrus clouds are high, wispy clouds. They form about 20,000 to 30,000 feet above the ground.

Cumulonimbus clouds are high, dark clouds. They form up to 60,000 feet above the ground. They often mean storms are coming.

People can observe clouds from the ground. Clouds are made up of water drops or bits of ice. There are different kinds of clouds. They are named for their shape, height, and distance above the ground. You can tell what the weather may be by looking at clouds. Dark clouds usually mean rain.

Weather Records

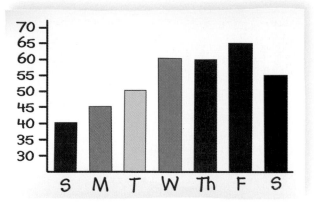

You can use a bar graph to record the daily high temperature in your area.

Forecasters often compare snow or rain amounts. They might make a weather chart to look at which towns got the greatest or least amount of snow. They use inches and feet to show how much snow or rain fell. They can compare these amounts to amounts recorded over many years. Then, they can tell if a storm was a record for an area.

Forecasters also record **extreme** weather. They keep track of the coldest and hottest temperatures. They record the fastest wind speed and the biggest piece of hail.

Weather Extremes in the United States

Kind of Weather	Place	Record
highest temperature	Death Valley, CA	134 degrees F
lowest temperature	Prospect Creek, AK	−80 degrees F
greatest rainfall	Alvin, TX	43 inches/1 day
greatest snowfall	Silver Lake, CO	76 inches/1 day
largest hailstone	Aurora, NE	7 inches wide
lowest yearly rain	Death Valley, CA	1.63 inches
greatest yearly rain	Kauai, HI	460 inches
longest time no rain	Bagdad, CA	767 days

Weather Maps

Weather maps give lots of useful information. They show the kind of weather in a large or a small area at a certain time.

A national weather map gives information about the whole country. The map is made from reports sent by weather stations. Thousands of weather measurements are put together into one big map.

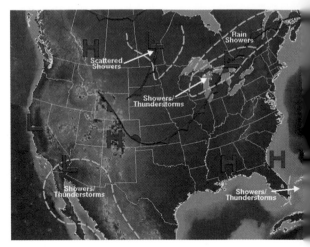

A national weather map is used to show current conditions and to predict the movement of weather for several days.

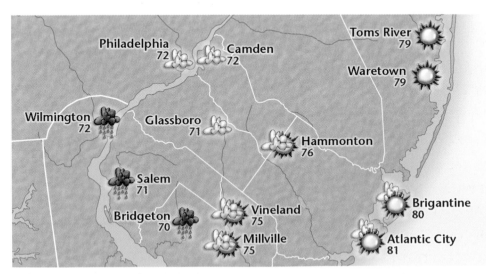

A local weather map shows details of what the weather is like or what it will be in a small area.

Weather maps use **symbols**. These symbols show different kinds of weather. There are symbols for rain, snow, sun, and wind. Many weather maps use color to show temperature. High or low pressure is shown with a large *H* or a large *L*.

Weather can be hard to predict. This is true no matter how much data the forecasters have. That is why they use words such as *maybe, a chance of,* and ***probable***.

A meteorologist uses maps and weather symbols to tell viewers what tomorrow's weather will be.

Percents in Weather

Did you ever hear a forecaster talk about weather in terms of percents? A percent is a fraction of 100. The closer a percent is to 100, the more likely the weather is to happen. A 90 percent (written as 90%) chance of rain means it is likely or almost certain that rain will fall on the whole area. What if there is a 20 percent chance of rain? Then, rain is less likely.

sunny   rain   snow

partly
cloudy   windy

some common weather symbols

13

Ever-Changing Weather

So much of what people do depends on the weather. You need to know if it will rain or be warm if you want to go swimming or on a picnic. You need to know if dangerous weather, such as a hurricane or tornado, is coming.

The weather is always changing. That's why meteorologists measure the weather often. They study all kinds of data. Then they have the best chance of giving people a correct forecast.

Weather forecasts can tell you if the weather is going to change.

Glossary

air pressure   the force of air pressing against Earth's surface

compare   to note the likeness or difference of

conditions   factors

data   facts that are gathered to get information

extreme   very great or strong; much more than usual

forecast   a prediction about the weather made after studying and examining data

humidity   the amount of water vapor in the air

orbit   to move in a circular path around something, such as Earth

probable   likely

radar   a system of radio signals or energy beams that reflect, or bounce off, raindrops, snowflakes, and other objects

record   to write; also the greatest of something, such as speed or amount

satellites   objects that have been put into orbit around Earth, the Moon, or another heavenly body

symbols   things that stand for other things

Index